SCRIBNER READING SERIES

MEET NEW FRIENDS

Jack Cassidy

Doris Roettger   *Karen K. Wixson*

SCRIBNER Laidlaw

New York

ACKNOWLEDGMENTS
Portions of this text have been adapted from materials
originally prepared under the direction of Dr. Charles Walcutt
and Dr. Glenn McCracken.
"Seesaw" is from ANOTHER HERE AND NOW STORY BOOK by Lucy
Sprague Mitchell. Copyright 1937 by E. P. Dutton, renewed
1965 by Lucy Sprague Mitchell. Reprinted by permission of
the publisher, E. P. Dutton, a division of New American
Library.

ILLUSTRATIONS
Cover: Cheryl Griesbach & Stanley Martucci.
Francoise Amadieu 26-29; Maxie Chambliss 40-41; Rick Cooley
45-49, 56-61; Len Ebert 81; Les Gray 42-44, 64-67, 78-80;
Meryl Henderson 16-20; Sal Murdocca 5-10, 50-55, 84-88;
Michele Noiset 21-25; Jerry Smath 11-15, 82, 83; N. Jo Smith
62, 63, 89-94; Samatha Smith 30-39; Linda Weller 68-72; Jane
Yamada 73-77.

SCRIBNER LAIDLAW
866 Third Avenue
New York, NY 10022
Collier Macmillan Canada, Inc.

Printed in the United States of America
ISBN 0-02-268880-3
9 8 7 6 5 4 3 2

Contents

The Campers

by Mike Thaler

It is summer.
It is hot.

5

Sam, Pippin, Ronda, and
Rumpus put up a tent.
Sam puts in a peg.
Pippin puts in a peg.
Ronda puts in a peg.
Rumpus puts in a peg.

Sam puts in a rod.
Pippin puts in a rod.
The tent sags.

Ronda tugs on the tent.
Rumpus tugs on the tent.
Ronda tugs hard.
Rumpus tugs harder.

The tent rips!

Sam mends the tent.

Sam gets in the tent.
It is fun.

Pippin gets in the tent.
It is fun.

Ronda gets in the tent.
It is fun.

Rumpus gets in the tent.
It is <u>not</u> fun!

The tent gets fat.
The tent gets fatter.
The tent rips!

Ronda is sad.
Sam is sadder.
Rumpus is saddest.

9

Sam cannot mend the tent.
He puts the tent on the grass.

Sam, Pippin, Ronda, and Rumpus
sit on the tent and rest
under the stars.

-ed added to words

hunt	dust	test	end
hunted	dusted	tested	ended
drift	start	dart	mend
drifted	started	darted	mended
pet	nod	spot	fit
petted	nodded	spotted	fitted

---

petted the cats
started to hum

A monster dusted the mats.
Ten monsters ■ the huts.

START THE SHOW

One hundred monsters sat in the sun.
One hundred monsters met for fun.

Ten rag monsters dusted the stars.
Ten fast monsters darted in cars.

12

Ten sad monsters mended the huts.
Ten red monsters hunted for nuts.

Ten fat monsters fed the cats.
Ten smart monsters sat on mats.

13

Ten egg monsters drifted in cups.
Ten hand monsters petted the pups.

Ten tin monsters tested a drum.
Ten mop monsters started to hum.

One hundred monsters sat in the sun.
One hundred monsters ended the fun.

One monster nodded to end the show.
One hundred monsters got up to go.

-ed added to words

dump	camp	pass	miss
dumped	camped	passed	missed

dip	mop	step	drop
dipped	mopped	stepped	dropped

hug	tag	pin	grin
hugged	tagged	pinned	grinned

---

dipped in
grinned at Dan

Greg dropped the egg.
Scott ■ up the mess.

FUN AT PEG'S

The fun at Peg's had started.
Peg dropped ●●● into a pan.
Scott had to dip in and get an ●.
He dipped in and got one out.
Scott and the ● dripped.

Amanda had a hard egg.
Dad said, "Get set, go!"

Amanda passed the egg fast to Pat.
Pat handed it fast to Greg.
Greg started to pass the egg
to Scott.
Greg missed.
He dropped the hard egg on the rug.

Peg handed Pat a hat and a pin.
Pat had to pin the hat on the cat.
Pat missed the cat.
She pinned the hat on the dog.

Pat handed Scott a hat and a pin.
Scott did it.
Scott pinned the hat on the cat.

Peg's mom and dad set out
the dinner.
Peg and Amanda passed the cups.

After dinner Scott, Pat, Amanda,
and Greg said, "Thanks, Peg."

W w

| wet | wind | win | won |
| went | winter | winner | wonder |

| wag | west | twin | swim |
| wagon | western | twig | swam |

---

in winter
swim in the

Winston won the contest.
The  got a red star.

A TRIP
TO THE STARS

Winston put a carpet on the grass.
His dog ran up to him.
The dog and Winston rested
on the carpet.
Winston and his dog had a nap.

The carpet started to go up.
It went past the garden.
The wind sent the carpet up past
a nest.
The carpet went up faster and faster.

A farmer stopped.
"Is it far to the stars?"
said Winston.

"It's not far," said the farmer.

"Thank you," said Winston.

The wagon and the carpet
started to go fast.
"A trip to the stars is fun,"
said Winston.

"ARF! ARF!" said his dog.

The wind stopped.
Winston's carpet started to drop.
It went past the nest and past
the garden.
The carpet dropped onto the grass.

Winston's dog got up.
It tugged on Winston's pants.

Winston sat up and hugged his dog.
His trip to the stars had ended.

Smart Coppertop

Marta has a pet hen.
Her hen is Coppertop.
Coppertop is a smart pet.

Marta has started a garden.
Coppertop can't go into the garden.
A hen can harm a garden.
Coppertop sits on the steps.

The sun is hot.
Marta must get her garden wet.
She gets a can to wet the garden.

Coppertop sees Marta.
Coppertop sees the garden.
She runs into the garden.

Marta drops the can and runs
after her!

Coppertop runs under Marta's wagon.
Marta runs after her.
Marta's western hat drops off.

A wind starts up.
It huffs and puffs.
The wind has Marta's hat.
The hat is up, up, up.

"Stop, hat, stop!" said Marta.

The hat stops on a twig.
Marta can't get it.
"Get the hat, Coppertop!"
"It's on the twig," said Marta.

Coppertop hops up on the twig.
The hen tugs and tugs on the hat.
The hat drops off the twig.

"Thank you," said Marta.
"You did it!"

w and a

want	wand	water
wanted	wander	watered

swan　　　swap

swamp　　swapped

---

seven swans
wanted to run

Emma and Wanda swapped hats.
One hat had a ▮ on it.

WATSON'S CAMP

It was summer.
Watson was sad.
His sister Emma was at camp.
Watson wanted to go to camp, too.

"I want to swim," said Watson.
"Emma gets to swim at camp."

"I want to pump water," said Watson.
"Emma gets to pump water at camp."

"I want a tent," said Watson.
"Emma gets a tent at camp."

"I want to go to camp," said Watson.

"You get to go to the farm," said Dad.
"Grandma wants to see you."

"The farm is not camp!" said Watson.
"Emma got to go to camp."

Watson went to the farm.

Grandma showed Watson the farm.
She showed him the pond.

"You can swim in the pond,
if you want to," said Grandma.

35

She showed him the pump.
"You can pump water for us,
if you want to," said Grandma.

She showed him a tent.
"You can put up the tent,
if you want to," said Grandma.

Grandma showed Watson her dog
Snuff.
Snuff had pups!
Grandma handed Watson a tan pup.

"The tan pup is for you,
if you want it," she said.

"The farm is fun!" said Watson.

Watson hugged his pup and grinned.
"Thank you, Grandma."

"I got a pup at the farm," he said.
"Emma can't get a pup at camp!"

THE ANTS

1 ant runs up
a camper's arm.

2 ants pump
the water
on a farm.

3 ants sit
in the hot sun
and sand.

4 ants dart
across the
farmer's hand.

5 ants wave
and go
to a show.

6 ants are sad.
The ants want
to go!

7 ants go
on a summer
trip.

8 ants swim
in the water
and drip.

w and ar

warn	warm
warns	warmer
warned	warmest

---

warns the man
warm in the summer

It is not warm in the car.
Get a ▮ hat.

IT WARNS YOU

This 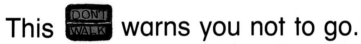 warns you not to go.

This warns cars not to go fast.

The warns you to stop.

The warns cars to stop, too.

The warns you
it must go fast!

aw in saw

saw	raw	straw	fawn
paw	draw	straws	dawn

---

paw prints

raw carrots

Edward got up at dawn.

He saw a tan

Paw Prints
on the Steps

Fran and Dennis run to the apartment.

They stop at the steps.

Dennis sees mud on the steps.

Fran sees paw prints.

The paw prints go up the steps.

Did a monster wander in?

Dennis and Fran run up the steps.

They run to Mr. Ward.
He has a mop in his hand.

"Did you see a monster go past?"
said Fran.

"Is it in the apartment?" said Dennis.

Mr. Ward grinned.
"I didn't see it," he said.
"I must mop up the mess."

The paw prints go on up the steps.
Dennis and Fran must warn Mom.

Fran and Dennis run up the steps.
They stop at the top.
The wet paw prints go on and on.

The monster is in the apartment!
Did the monster harm Mom?
Can the monster harm us?

Fran and Dennis run into the apartment.

The monster is in the apartment.
It is a dog.
It has mud on its paws!

The monster is Moppet.
Moppet is a gift for Dennis and Fran.
They thank Mom and hug her.
They hug Moppet the monster, too!

L l

leg	let	left	last
log	lit	lift	lost
flag	plan	lap	held
flap	plant	clap	help

lost the list

flap in the wind

Len can plant a garden.

Lil can ▇ him.

THE FLAG

by Mike Thaler

Sam, Pippin, Ronda, and Rumpus
wanted a flag.

"I can draw it," said Sam.

"Can you draw stars?" said Rumpus.

"Draw stars," said Pippin.

"Yes, draw stars!" said Ronda.

Sam started to draw a star.

"Show us the star!" said Rumpus.

Sam held it up.

"No, no," said Ronda.

"A star has tips," said Pippin.
"You must add tips."

Sam started to draw tips.

"Now show us the star," said Rumpus.

Sam held it up.

"No, no," said Ronda.

"Now the star has lumps!" said Pippin.

"A star is hard to draw," said Sam.

"I want to draw different stars," said Sam.
Sam started to draw.

"Let us see the flag," said Rumpus.

"Not now," said Sam.

"I want to see the flag!" said Pippin.

"Not now," said Sam.

"Show us the flag," said Ronda.

"You can see it now," said Sam.

Sam handed the flag to Ronda.
She held the flag up.
It flapped and fluttered in the wind.

"You put <u>us</u> on the flag!"
said Rumpus.

"Yes," said Sam.
"I put the top stars on the flag."

"It is a grand flag!" said Pippin.

"It is a flag of stars!" said Ronda.

And it was.

ll in hill

hill	fill	sell	well
will	still	tell	swell

hall	fall	wall	full
tall	call	small	pull

---

a small dog
will go

Dennis can pull the wagon.
The wagon will go up the ▊.

Up the Hill

Dennis has a car.
It is red.
His car can go fast.
To start his car, Dennis
has to press the pedal.

It is after supper.
Fran, Dennis, and Moppet sit
on the steps.

57

"Let's go up the hill," said Dennis.

"No, I want to rest," said Fran.

Dennis said, "You sit in the wagon.
I will get in the car.
The car will pull you.
You can rest and still go up the hill."

Dennis got in the car.
Fran got in the wagon and held on.

Moppet ran up to her.
"Arf, arf," he said.

"Moppet wants to get in the wagon,"
said Fran.

"Well, tell him he can't get in,"
said Dennis.
"I can't pull you <u>and</u> Moppet."

Dennis pressed the pedal.
The car started up the hill.
U . . . p, u . . . p went the car.
It stopped.

"I can't get the car to the top,"
said Dennis.

Moppet ran up the hill to Fran.
"Arf, arf," he said.

"Moppet wants to help," said Fran.
"He wants to pull us up the hill."

Moppet pulled the car and the wagon.
He got to the top of the hill.
"Arf, arf," said Moppet.

"He wants to get in the wagon,"
said Fran.

"Tell him he can get in now,"
said Dennis.

Moppet got in.

"Let's go!" called Fran.

Moppet had a grand trip.

ow in now

now	cow	gown
how	crowd	down
wow	crowded	downtown
flower	clown	drown
tower	crown	frown

---

up and down
a red flower

Howard saw a clown.
The clown had on a .

SEESAW

by Evelyn Beyer

Up and down,
Up and down,
Seesaws pop
Up,
Seesaws drop
Down.

The down is a bump,
The up is a jump.
See-saw,
See-saw,
UP!

Downtown to the Tower

Papa and I went downtown.
We wanted to see the tower.
I wanted to go up to the top of it.

We passed tall apartments.
We saw crowds and lots of cars.

Papa frowned.
"It's too crowded," he said.
"I will stop the car and we can
get out."

Papa and I stepped into the crowds.
We stopped at a flower stand.

We saw flags flap in the wind.

We saw a clown in a tall hat.
She put a crown on me.

At last we saw the tower.
It had tall, tall walls of glass.

"I can't see the top of the tower,"
I said.

Papa and I went up, up, up.

"We are at the top now,"
said Papa.
The wind tugged hard at us.
I held Papa's hand.

From the top we saw downtown and
the water, too.

"See how small the crowd is now!"
said Papa.

He showed me a map
of downtown.
I saw it all from the top
of the tower.

"Wow!" I said to Papa.
"It's fun to go up and see down."

B b

bus	bed	barn
big	bad	bottom
bigger	bat	best
biggest	batter	better
number	rub	grab
member	club	grabbed

---

on a bus
on the bottom

Bob's bat is big.
But Bill's bat is .

The Smartest Batter

Bob is on Mr. Wilson's ball club.
The club is called the 3-Bs.
The 3-Bs stands for Better
Batter Ball Club.
Bob's pals go to the club, too.
They go to Mr. Wilson's farm in a bus.

Bob is not a bad hitter.
He bats well and runs fast.
But his pal, Len, is better.
Len is the best hitter on the club.

69

Last summer, Len hit a ball hard.
The ball went past Mr. Wilson's cows.
It went past Mr. Wilson's garden.

Bob missed the ball.
It landed far up the hill.
Bob had to run after it.

At last the ball stopped.
It stopped in Mr. Wilson's pig pen.

Bob spotted the ball in the pen.
But he had a problem.
The pen was full of big pigs.

The biggest pig saw the ball.
The pig grabbed it.

Bob must not go into the pig pen.
How will he get the ball?

Bob ran fast to Mr. Wilson's garden.
He pulled up a carrot and ran to
the pig pen.

The big pig still had the ball.
Bob held the carrot in front of the pig.

It dropped the ball and grabbed
the carrot.
Bob grabbed the ball and held it up.
The 3-Bs hollered and clapped.

Len is the best batter.
But Bob is the smartest member of
the Better Batter Ball Club.

le in **apple**

apple	puddle	little
apples	cuddle	bottle

riddle	giggle
middle	bubble

handle	sample	grumble
candle	dimple	stumble

---

sat in the middle
had lots of apples

Deb has a little sister.
Deb will hug and ■ her.

BIG SISTER

Deb held her dad's hand.
Mom was down the hall in 204.
Deb saw the number on the wall.
Deb and her dad went in.

Mom saw Deb and held up her arms.
Mom was glad to hug Deb!
"How are you?" said Mom.
"I missed you.
You are a big sister now."

Deb grinned and hugged her mom.

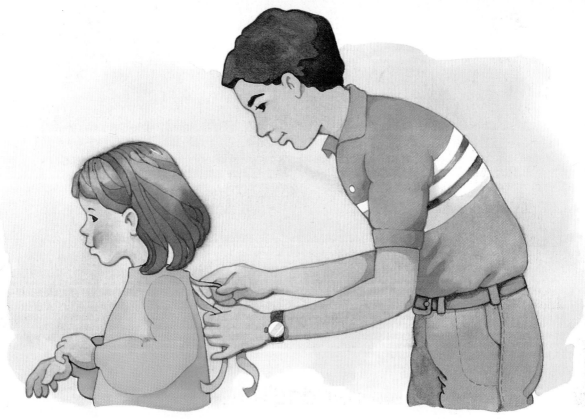

Donna was in a small crib.
Deb wanted to hug her little sister.

Dad helped Deb scrub her hands.
He helped her put on a gown.

Deb sat down.
Mom put Donna on Deb's lap.
Deb cuddled her little sister.
Deb's hand held Donna's small hand.

Dad got a bottle of water.
Deb handed Donna to her dad.

Dad fed Donna the bottle of water.
He patted Donna to get up a bubble.

"You will help get the bottles,"
Mom said to Deb.
"You can help me a lot."

Mom cuddled Deb, and Dad
held Donna.
Deb was glad she was a big sister.
Mom still had lots of hugs
for her.

77

How To
Start a Bottle Garden

A garden in a bottle is fun.
It is not hard for you to start.

1. Get a little bottle.

2. Get small bags of sand.
Get red, tan, and
brown sand.

3. Now put red sand
in the bottom
of the bottle.

4. Add tan sand on top of the red sand.

5. Add brown sand on top of the tan sand.

6. Add red sand to fill the bottle.

7. Now, put a little plant
in the middle.
A cactus is the best.
Press the sand down.

8. Put a little water
on the plant.
Lots of water is bad
for a cactus.

Now it's a garden in a bottle!

K k

kid	kept	skip
kitten	kettle	skin
ask	desk	bark
mask	dark	mark
basket	park	market

---

at the market
in the park

Kim had a little kitten.
The kitten slept in a .

81

gas truck

ck in duck

duck	sock	stick
luck	lock	click
truck	clock	trick
pick	pack	rack
pickle	back	stack
pocket	black	cracker

---

in the back
in her pocket

We put ten big bottles of pickles
in the back of the ▮.

milk truck

dump truck

TRUCKS, TRUCKS, TRUCKS

If you go on a trip, you will see
lots of different trucks.
Six different trucks are in the picture.
Can you add to the list?

cattle truck

pickup truck

log truck

Supper for Pippin

by Mike Thaler

"Let's go on a picnic!" said Sam.

"Yes, yes, yes," said Rumpus, Ronda, and Pippin.

Sam got the picnic basket.

"I will pack apples," said Sam.

"Yes, yes," said Rumpus and Ronda.

"Not for me," said Pippin.

"I will pack pickles," said Sam.

"Yes, yes," said Rumpus and Ronda.

"Not for me," said Pippin.

"I will pack hot dogs and buns,"
said Sam.

"Yes, yes," said Rumpus and Ronda.

"Not for me," said Pippin.

"I will pack nuts for you," said Sam.

"No nuts for me," said Pippin.

"Pack nuts for us," said Rumpus and Ronda.

Sam packed the basket, and they went to a grand spot.

Sam, Rumpus, and Ronda had
apples,
pickles,
hot dogs,
buns, and
nuts
for supper.

Pippin did not.

87

Ants ran up.

"Bad luck!" said Sam.

"Awful!" said Ronda.

"Pests!" said Rumpus.

"Supper!" said Pippin.

Pippin grinned,
and puckered,
and picked up all the ants.

nk in sink

sink	bank	hunk	blink
pink	sank	bunk	blinked

wink	tank	skunk	blank
drink	drank	trunk	blanket

---

in the bank
in the sink

Get a warm blanket for the bed.
The blanket is in the ▮.

The
Lost Blanket

Linda has a cat and a dog.

She calls her cat Nutmeg.

She calls her dog Topper.

Topper lets the cat drink milk

from his pan.

Nutmeg and Topper are pals.

Topper slept on a blanket at
the bottom of Linda's bunk bed.
He slept on it in the car, too.

But now the blanket was not
on the bed.
It was lost.

Linda's mom was at the sink.
"Linda," she said, "is Topper's
blanket <u>under</u> the bunk bed?"

It was not under the bunk bed.

"Is it in the car trunk?" asked Dad.

It was not in the car trunk.

"Is Topper's blanket in the attic?"
asked Uncle Frank.

It was not in the attic.

Linda hunted up and down the farm.
But she didn't see Topper's blanket.

Linda and Topper sat down
on the back steps.

Linda's dad was up at the barn.
He waved and called to her.

Linda and Topper ran to the barn.

"Go up to the loft," said Dad.

Linda crept up the steps to the
dark loft.
Topper went past her.
He ran to the back of the loft and
started to bark.

"Bow wow! Bow wow wow!" barked
Topper.

Topper's blanket was in the straw.
On top of the blanket was Nutmeg.
She had one little kitten cuddled up
to her.

Linda picked up the little kitten.
She sat down in front of Topper.
Topper sniffed and licked the kitten.
He licked Nutmeg, too.

Dad said, "Topper is glad.
He is glad his pal Nutmeg had
his lost blanket."

Story Vocabulary

Story Vocabulary